GERMAN SHEPHERD
VIRTUES

GERMAN SHEPHERD
VIRTUES

Lessons Learned From Our Faithful Companions

Compiled By Melissa Sovey

■ WILLOW CREEK PRESS

Published by Willow Creek Press
P.O. Box 147, Minocqua, Wisconsin 54548

Photo Credits:
p2: © Juniors Bildarchiv/agefotostock.com; p5 © Richard Stacks/Kimball Stock;
p6-7 © Tim Ridley/agefotostock.com; p8 © J.M. Labat/ardea.com; p11,12 © Juniors Bildarchiv/agefotostock.com;
p15 © Tara Gregg/Sporthorse Photography; p16,19 © Juniors Bildarchiv/agefotostock.com;
p 20 © Close Encounters of the Fury Kind/Kimball Stock; p22-23 © Juniors Bildarchiv/agefotostock.com;
p24 © ARCO/P. Wegner/agefotostock.com; p27 © Nick Ridley/Kimball Stock; p28-29 © Tara Gregg/Sporthorse Photography;
p31 © Johan De Meester/ardea.com; p32,35 © Ron Kimball/Kimball Stock; p36 © ARCO/P. Wegner/agefotostock.com;
p38-39 © Erich Kuchling/agefotostock.com; p40 © J.M. Labat/ardea.com; p43 © Tara Gregg/Sporthorse Photography;
p44 © Beverly Logan/agefotostock.com; p47 © Huetter, C./agefotostock.com; p48 © J.M. Labat/ardea.com;
p51,52 © Juniors Bildarchiv/agefotostock.com; p55 © ARCO/P. Wegner/agefotostock.com; p56 © Klein-Hubert/Kimball Stock;
p58-59 © Ron Kimball/Kimball Stock; p60 © Tara Gregg/Sporthorse Photography; p63 © John Foxx/agefotostock.com;
p64-65 © Ron Kimball/Kimball Stock; p67 © Renee Stockdale/Kimball Stock; p68 © Ron Kimball/Kimball Stock;
p70,71 © Juniors Bildarchiv/agefotostock.com; p72 © Freiburg, S./agefotostock.com; p75 © Alberto Ramella/agefotostock.com;
p76 © Juniors Bildarchiv/agefotostock.com; p79 © J.M. Labat/ardea.com; p80 © ARCO/P. Wegner/agefotostock.com;
p83 © Juniors Bildarchiv/agefotostock.com; p84 © J.M. Labat/ardea.com; p87 © Nick Ridley/Kimball Stock;
p88-89,91-92 © Ron Kimball/Kimball Stock; p95 © Gary Randall/Kimball Stock;

Excerpt Acknowledgements:
p18 France, Anatole. *The Amethyst Ring*; a translation by B. Drillien. London; New York: John Lane, 1919.
p73,86 Houston, Pam. *Sight Hound*. New York: W.W. Norton, 2005.

Design: Donnie Rubo
Printed in Canada

THERE ARE CERTAIN CHARACTERISTICS WE FIND HONORABLE in each other and valuable to leading a good life. We call these characteristics virtues. We search for ways to cultivate strength in character through example, and through effort and will, always seeking the most effective teacher. It might be said that the degree to which we attain these virtues influences our very spirit.

Perhaps the perfect teacher doesn't have to think about attaining these virtues, but instead innately lives with a reverence for life in every aspect of play, and in service and friendship. The German Shepherd, by its very nature, guides us in these life lessons. Through demeanor and deeds, the German Shepherd shows us that leading the "good life" is invigorating and fulfilling. This book is a tribute to the breed, and to all dogs, whose joy and devotion to being alive inspires the virtuous in all of us.

—*Melissa Sovey*

"We expect our dogs to listen to us
when we speak to them and our dogs, no
less than we, do expect us to listen to them."

—Roger Caras

ATTENTIVENESS

Lots of people talk to animals...
not very many listen, though.
That's the problem."

—Benjamin Hoff

"The dog has no ambition, no self-interest, no desire for vengeance, no fear other than that of displeasing."

—*George-Louis Leclerc, Comte de Buffon*

BRAVERY

"One isn't necessarily born with courage, but one is born with potential. Without courage, we cannot practice any other virtue with consistency. We can't be kind, true, merciful, generous, or honest."

—*Maya Angelou*

"The psychological and moral comfort
of a presence at once humble and
understanding—this is the greatest benefit
that the dog has bestowed upon man."

—*Percy Bysshe Shelley*

CARING

"Virtue does not always demand a heavy sacrifice,
only the willingness to make it when necessary."

—*Frederick Sherwood Dunn*

"If we lack confidence in ourselves and our relationship
with our dogs, we communicate that to them...
in countless subtle and not-so-subtle ways."

—Myrna Milani, D.V.M.

CONFIDENCE

"Have patience with all things, but chiefly have patience
with yourself. Do not lose courage in considering your
own imperfections, but instantly set about remedying
them—every day begin the task anew."

—Saint Francis de Sales

"Animals are such agreeable friends—they
ask no questions, they pass no criticisms."

—*George Eliot*

COOPERATION

"Virtue is not knowing, but doing."

—*Japanese proverb*

"Dog!

When we first met on the highway of life,

we came from the two poles of creation.

What can be the meaning of the obscure love

for me that has sprung up in your heart?"

From The Amethyst Ring *by Anatole France*

CURIOSITY

"Curiosity is the one thing invincible in Nature."

—*Freya Stark*

"Dogs are wonderful. Truly.
To know them and be with them
is an experience that transcends—
a way to understand the joyfulness
of living and devotion."

—*Gary Paulsen*

DEVOTION

"Only my dogs will not betray me."

—*Maria Callas*

DISCIPLINE

"We derive immeasurable good,
uncounted pleasures,
enormous security,
and many critical lessons
about life by owning dogs."

—Roger Caras

"I love a dog.

He does nothing for political reasons."

—Will Rogers

DUTY

"Our real duty is always found running in

the direction of our worthiest desires."

—Randolph S. Bourne

"He suffered from a suppressed, or better, superfluity of unemployed energy; for he was in heaven when someone was occupied with him, and he was then the most tractable of dogs."

—*Max Von Stephanitz*

EAGERNESS

"There is no genius in life like the genius of energy and industry."

—*Don G. Mitchell*

"Man himself cannot express love and humility by external signs so plainly as does a dog, when with dropping ears, hanging lips, flexuous body, and wagging tail, he meets his beloved master."

—*Charles Darwin*

FAITHFULNESS

"My dogs forgive anger in me, the arrogance in me, the brute in me. They forgive everything I do before I forgive myself."

—*Guy de la Valdene*

FORGIVENESS

"True forgiveness includes total acceptance."

—*Catherine Marshall*

"You ask of my companions. Hills, sir, and the sundown, and a dog as large as myself that my father bought me. They are better than human beings, because they know but do not tell."

—*Emily Dickinson*

FRIENDLINESS

"Sincerity is the way of Heaven."

—*Mencius*

"The dog of your boyhood teaches you a great deal about friendship, and love, and death: old Skip was my brother."

—*Willie Morris*

GENTLENESS

"There is nothing stronger in the world than gentleness."

—*Han Suyin*

"With no concept of beginnings or endings dogs probably don't know that for people having a dog as a life companion provides a streak of light between two eternities of darkness."

—*Stanley Coren*

GRACE

"I do not understand the mystery of grace— only that it meets us where we are, but does not leave us where it found us."

—*Anne Lamott*

"I can't think of anything that brings me closer to tears than when my old dog—completely exhausted after a hard day in the field—limps away from her nice spot in front of the fire and comes over to where I'm sitting and puts her head in my lap, a paw over my knee, and closes her eyes, and goes back to sleep. I don't know what I've done to deserve that kind of friend."

—*Gene Hill*

GRATITUDE

"A thankful heart is not only the greatest virtue, but the parent of all other virtues."

—*Marcus Tullius Cicero*

"He is your friend, your partner, your defender, your dog.
You are his life, his love, his leader. He will be yours,
faithful and true, to the last beat of his heart.
You owe it to him to be worthy of such devotion."

—*Anonymous*

GUARDIANSHIP

"Loyalty means nothing unless it has at its
heart the absolute principle of self-sacrifice."

—*Woodrow T. Wilson*

"This soldier... lay there deserted by all except his dog.
I looked on, unmoved, at battles which decided the future
of nations. Tearless, I had given orders which brought death
to thousands. Yet here I was stirred, profoundly stirred,
stirred to tears. And by what? By the grief of one dog."

—*Napoleon Bonaparte*

HONOR

"Dignity does not consist in possessing
honors, but in deserving them."

—*Aristotle*

"The dogs in our lives, the dogs we come to love and who (we fervently believe) love us in return, offer more than fidelity, consolation, and companionship. They offer comedy, irony, wit, and a wealth of anecdotes..."

—*Marjorie Garber*

HUMOR

"Humor is to the soul what rain is to the Earth."

—*Gerry Hopman*

"His courage, his fidelity, and the degree in which he often devotes every power that he possesses to our service, are circumstances that we can never forget nor overlook."

—*William Youatt*

INTEGRITY

"Virtues are acquired through endeavor, which rests wholly upon yourself."

—*Sidney Lanier*

"It is often a matter of the inherent tending instinct with the shepherd dog, who is not working with the flocks, which makes him take care of other living beings in his own way, to gather them together, to fend for them, but also not to allow anything to be done in contravention of law and order, according to his own private interpretation of what that is."

—*Max Von Stephanitz*

JUSTICE

"All virtue is summed up in dealing justly."

—*Aristotle*

"...she would launch into a celebratory dance that ended with her racing around the room, always clockwise, and faster and faster, as if her joy could not be possibly contained. Even as a young boy I knew that hardly any creature could express joy so vividly as a dog."

—*Jeffrey Moussaieff Masson*

JOYFULNESS

"Those who bring sunshine into the lives of others cannot keep it from themselves."

—*James M. Barrie*

"Of the memory of the dog, and the recollection of kindness received, there are a thousand stories, from the return of Ulysses to the present day, and we have seen enough of that faithful animal to believe most of them."

—*William Youatt*

KINDNESS

"Remember there's no such thing as a small act of kindness. Every act creates a ripple with no logical end."

—*Scott Adams*

"No one can fully understand the meaning of love unless he's owned a dog. A dog can show you more honest affection with a flick of his tail than a man can gather through a lifetime of handshakes."

—*Gene Hill*

LOVE

"Love is that which exists to do good, not merely to get good."

—*Victoria Woodhull*

"The fidelity of a dog is a precious gift demanding no less binding moral responsibilities than the friendship of a human being. The bond with a true dog is as lasting as the ties of this earth can ever be."

—*Konrad Lorenz*

LOYALTY

"Unless you can find some sort of loyalty, you cannot find unity and peace in your active living."

—*Josiah Royce*

MAJESTY

"He possessed beauty without vanity, strength
without insolence; courage without ferocity;
and all the virtues of man without his vices."

—*Lord Byron*

"Dogs travel hundreds of miles during their lifetime responding to such commands as 'come' and 'fetch'."
—*Stephen Baker*

OBEDIENCE

"A great work is made out of a combination of obedience and liberty."
—*Nadia Boulanger*

"I can still see my first dog.
For six years he met me at the same place
after school and convoyed me home—
a service he thought up himself.
A boy doesn't forget that sort of association."

—E.B. White

PATIENCE

"Patience is not passive; on the contrary,
it is active; it is concentrated strength."

—Edward Bulwer-Lytton

"Both humans and dogs love to play well into adulthood, and individuals from both species occasionally display evidence of having a conscience."

—*John Winokur*

PLAYFULNESS

"A shepherd may be a very able, trusty, and good shepherd without a sweetheart—better, perhaps, than with one. But what is he without his dog?"

—*James Hogg*

PURPOSEFULNESS

"The soul which has no fixed purpose in life is lost; to be everywhere, is to be nowhere."

—*Michel de Montaigne*

"The dog was cold and in pain.
But being only a dog it did not occur
to him to trot off home to the comfort
of the library fire and leave his
master to fend for himself."

—*Albert Payson Terhune*

RELIABILITY

"A good man will take care of his horses
and dogs, not only while they are young,
but also when old and past service."

—*Plutarch*

RESPECT

"As I get older, I feel myself becoming more and more a dog, and I feel my dog becoming more and more an aristocrat."

—*Paul Claudel*

"After all, aren't we all just trying to learn the same things here, about sharing the food bowl with our sisters and brothers, trying to keep the crumbs out of the dog bed, remembering to bring the squeaky toys inside in case of rain?"

From Sight Hound *by Pam Houston*

RESPONSIBILITY

"Nothing strengthens the judgment and quickens the conscience like individual responsibility."

—*Elizabeth Cady Stanton*

"I have found that when you are deeply troubled, there are things you get from the silent devoted companionship of a dog that you can get from no other source."

—*Doris Day*

SENSITIVITY

"We cannot live for ourselves alone. Our lives are connected by a thousand invisible threads, and along these sympathetic fibers, our actions run as causes and return to us as results."

—*Herman Melville*

"The dog has been esteemed and loved by all
the people on earth and he has deserved this
affection for he renders services that have
made him man's best friend."

—*Alfred Barbou*

SERVICE

"I don't know what your destiny will be,
but one thing I do know: the only ones
among you who will be really happy are those
who have sought and found how to serve."

—*Albert Schweitzer*

"My dog is usually pleased with what I do, because she is not infected with the concept of what I 'should' be doing."

—*Lonzo Idolswine*

SPONTANEITY

"Analysis kills spontaneity. The grain once ground into flour springs and germinates no more."

—*Henri Frederic Amiel*

"I know that I have had friends who would
never have vexed or betrayed me,
if they had walked on all fours."

—*Horace Walpole*

STEADFASTNESS

"Fortitude is the guard and support
of the other virtues."

—*John Locke*

"It is true that whenever a person loves a
dog he derives great power from it."

—*Old Seneca Chief*

STRENGTH

"Being deeply loved by someone gives you strength,
while loving someone deeply gives you courage."

—*Lao Tzu*

"We long for an affection altogether ignorant of our faults. Heaven has accorded this to us in the uncritical canine attachment."

—*George Eliot*

TOLERANCE

"Out beyond ideas of wrongdoing and rightdoing, there is a field. I will meet you there."

—*Rumi*

"Even as a puppy he would worry about his toys; when they squeaked or rattled he seemed to think they were in some kind of pain, and he would bring them all onto his bagel bed, stare over them with those eyebrows of his going up and down, and nuzzle but never chew them."

From Sight Hound *by Pam Houston*

TRUSTWORTHINESS

"I agree with Agassiz that dogs possess something very much like a conscience."

—Charles Darwin

"He is my other eyes that can see above the clouds;
my other ears that hear above the winds. He is the part of
me that can reach out into the sea. He has told me a thousand
times over that I am his reason for being; by the way he rests
against my leg; by the way he thumps his tail at my smallest smile;
by the way he shows his hurt when I leave without taking him."

—*Gene Hill*

"A dog can have a friend; he has affections and character,
he can enjoy equally the field and the fireside; he dreams,
he caresses, he propitiates; he offends, and is pardoned;
he stands by you in adversity; he is a good fellow."

—*Leigh Hunt*

VERSATILITY

"He is blessed over all mortals who
loses no moment of the passing life."

—*Henry David Thoreau*

"At this particular moment I was allowed
to see infinity through my dog's eyes,
and I was old enough to know that.
They were as deep, as bewildering,
as unattainable as a night sky."

—*Meinrad Craighead*

WISDOM

"My description of wisdom has nothing
to do with benevolence and righteousness,
it is to do with being wise in one's
own virtue, nothing more."

—*Chuang Tzu*

"Both powerfully imaginary and comfortingly real, dogs act as mirrors for our own beliefs about what would constitute a truly humane society. Perhaps it is not too late for them to teach us some new tricks."

—*Marjorie Garber*

WONDER

"The few wonders of the world only exist while there are those with the sight to see them."

—*Charles de Lint*